These Several Women

Love Poems

Also by Cristina L. White

Sex and Soul
A Memoir of Salvation
Letter Pen Press

The Enchanted Journey
A play for children
Samuel French, Inc.

The Healing Environment
(Authored as Cristina Ismael)
Celestial Arts

These Several Women

Love Poems

Cristina Luisa White

LETTER
P·E·N
PRESS

Corvallis, Oregon

These Several Women: Love Poems

Copyright © 2018 by Cristina L. White
Published by Letter Pen Press, Corvallis, Oregon

All rights reserved. This book may not be reproduced in whole or in part, in any form or by any electronic or mechanical means, without written permission from the author, except by a reviewer, who may quote brief passages in a review. Any member of an educational institution wishing to photocopy part or all of this work for classroom use, or anthology, should contact the author at www.cristinalwhite.com. Thank you for your support of the author's rights.

Cover and interior design by Ray Rhamey

Library of Congress Control Number: 2018913885

ISBN 978-09906261-3-8

Printed in the United States of America

From first love to last, and with boundless gratitude,
I dedicate these poems to the women
who inspired them.

Acknowledgments

As a young adult I came across *Configurations* by Octavio Paz. I opened the book to "Sun Stone" and fell into poetry, fell in love with a poet. Here was language that set the page afire, startled the mind, carried me heart and soul to new dimensions. It was that experience that led me to more fully explore the world of poets and poetry. It also marked my first attempts at writing poetry.

Over time, I've discovered numerous poets whose work I admire. Of these, there are only a few I read again and again. In recent years, I most often turn to Billy Collins, Mary Oliver, and the *haiku* of Basho, Buson, and Issa. And there are other poets—perhaps not so widely known—whose poems inspire, enlighten, and help my understanding of the human heart. Their poems capture the light and dark of our shared, mysterious journey here on earth. I keep close, and return often, to these slender volumes: *Short Poems* by Rachel Barton, *Collected Poems* by Elizabeth Carlson, *Hubba Hubba* by Katherine Harer, *the day is ready for you* by Alison Malee, *Sand* by Michael Marsh, *Faith in the Color Turquoise* by Marjorie Power, *Held in the Weave* by Suzanne Sigafoos, and *The Season of Distress and Clarity* by Doug Stone.

A few of these poets I know, others I may never meet. I thank them all for their work.

And I thank, ever and always, Donna Jayne, my first reader and the sounding board for all my writing. She is unfailingly honest and keeps me true. She is the prose and poetry, letter, line and light of all my days and nights.

Contents

If Ever	1
New York	3
Remnants	4
I Knew	5
San Francisco	7
Strawberries	8
After the Cinema	11
Kindness, Only Remembered	14
The Shadow of the Roses	17
Sonoma	23
Chapters	24
Remembering	30
Stephanie	31
That Time We Argued	32
Amen	34
Fated	35
After Midnight	36
LosAngeles, San Francisco, Corvallis	38
The Mighty Pen	39

Coda 41
Final Farewell 42

If Ever

If ever my thumb should heal
and I can hold a pen again,
I will write poems
and next to them,
drawings in brown ink.

I will draw everything I see
and all my poems
will be about you.

New York

Remnants

Clear sea green cologne,
dusty paper flowers,
a string of tiny bells.

Everywhere I look
(I look everywhere,
anywhere, to avoid her eyes)
I find remnants
of an old affair.

I Knew

I knew the first time I saw you
alone on a stage
singing a medieval ballad,
your voice high, and pure, and clear.

I knew the first time we spoke
in a room crowded with people,
amidst all the chatter and laughter, we found
a corner where we could hear each other;
we talked for hours,
reluctant to part
even when it was near dawn.

You must have known
that bright, sunlit day
when I tapped out a rhythmic beat
on your door, danced along the walkway
and sang, come out, come out and play,
it's beautiful. But you couldn't,
so I stayed indoors, kept you company
even when all the world was intoxicated
by the light, the air, spring,

I stayed with you.
It wasn't until the eve of my departure,
my suitcase already packed,
when you came to say good-bye,
not until then did we admit what we both knew.

We sat together on the floor,
our backs against a white-washed wall.
The glow of twilight
became an indistinct dark, and neither of us
moved to turn on the lamp. After a long silence
you said, "I think I'm in love with you."

I took your hand and held it in mine
and wondered why we waited this long,
but of course neither of us wanted to want
what everyone had told us it was wrong to want.
And so, we tried, all this time, from our first meeting,
not to want, want, want
the only love we really wanted.

On the long trip away from you,
I thought about that rain-soaked night
when I had to see you, had to talk to you,
and you opened the door, half-asleep.
You drew me toward you, brought me inside,
no questions asked, you drew me to you, soft,
soft, soft,
and I knew.

San Francisco

Strawberries

We are in a deep,
    hot
        bath
and you take
    a strawberry
    from the china dish
    carefully placed on
    candle-lit wood
you
    bite into the ripe red
    strawberry heart
we
    pass the fruit between us
    with our tongues
    in a
        long strawberry kiss
and you
    caress
        my shoulder, my neck
        with the cold, sweet
        strawberry flesh

I take
>	another strawberry
>	another bite
>	and sink
>>		into
>>		one more kiss

I say
>	you know
>	we're leading
>>		to the inevitable

you say
>	you mean
>>		dying of pleasure?

And I say
>	nothing
>>		I kiss you
>>		and caress your breasts
>>		with the cool, succulent, secret
>>		strawberry tissue

We linger
>	the strawberry and I
>	upon your soft, sighing
>>		belly

I   pass the fruit   gently
>	between your thighs
>	squeeze and push gently

```
you
      are moaning        gently
         oh no   oh no   oh no
and I
      know
      you mean
               oh yes
                            oh yes
                                      oh
```

After the Cinema

After the cinema,
in the late afternoon, on a cold spring day,
we drive to the Marina,
to a class where you study French,
and at the doorway of an old stone building,
you wave, farewell, adieu.
You turn, walk away, and though you are gone
from sight, you are with me still.
I am lost
in you, in love, in a story we write
with breath and touch, in a language
we keep only for each other.

In the late afternoon, on a cold spring day,
I dream I am an elegant thief,
a lavish romantic, and you, my lover, evocation of love,
with pale blue eyes, copper red burnt red sheen red hair,
and I am snow falling, white flowers
falling snow flowers floating, and we are adrift
in a deep green meadow
where a thousand soft white flowers
are bedding us down, down,
in the sacred arc of our loving.

I want to sleep in a feather bed with you on feather pillows
with white ostrich feathers to brush your fair, soft skin
in a long, soft caress of unearthly soft down feathers
and then, maybe then,
there will be time
to sink into every crevice and curve of your body.

In the late afternoon, on a cold spring day,
I dream there is only your body, and mine,
we disappear
into each other.
You are velvet and silk, luxurious elixir,
I am the depth of my dreams
creating a woman who has your eyes
and your face, who has your graceful throat and your shoulders
sloping down to breasts that curve quietly as your breasts
swell
gently
a woman with your hands whose touch is so loving,
so tender, I quiver open opening into a vein where trust flows
and you call my name in the night ride
we take on wave upon wave of an incandescent ecstasy.

We are liquid becoming water becoming rain
river flowing into ocean,
a deep sweet infinity
holding us in this moment where light spills
on lovers and we are holy because we are lovers,

we are loving, we are love,
love cloaked in beautiful bodies sleeping dreaming
waking to the radiant storm of our loving in an era
known as San Francisco changing into you and I
loving.

Kindness, Only Remembered

Morning. I look up from the dark soil
of my garden, up from seeding,
singing the seeds
to the life they will become,
I look up and out
to the city.

San Francisco is awake.
The fog is receding, the streets are trafficking.
People shop, drink coffee,
make deals, scheme,
dream
skyscrapers and paper empires.

Somewhere
out there
lovers press together for one more embrace,
the unemployed cluster in long lines,
collect money, wonder how they will live.
A boy struggles with a poem,
an old woman completes a sentence,
a child is playing, another is crying,
a car breaks down.

My friend Joe drinks tea
and considers last night's dream.
In North Beach, an old man with a white moustache
makes a perfect cappuccino. A mother in a renovated flat
does not take time to shape the question,
how will I get through the day?

Somewhere
in this urban landscape
you are rising out of sleep into
today's explanations,
or perhaps you are
still held fast in a dream,
wrapped in the warmth of the burly man
who loves you. I brush that image aside
and see you alone, walking along a city street,
the sun and shadow play
catching the copper glint
light in your hair.

I am here, my feet firmly planted
in the wealth of my garden, here
above the cityscene, wondering
if we will ever recapture
the innocence of Wednesday
when the sky was a perfect blue, the sun
was warm and I showed you
the wild radish on the hill.

A day of stray white clouds
and endless ocean
when I
still thought kindly
of your other lover.

The Shadow of the Roses

Wednesday. Why, I wonder, is it so often Wednesday
when these great events
take place for us?
There was a rainbow Wednesday
when we stretched out beneath the trees,
near the lake, near the blue ice
cream sky. I felt the warmth of your hand
holding mine, our bed of soft grass, my own
happiness. We spoke of our families,
and lunched on miners lettuce.
We were jobless, there was nowhere
we had to be; we were content.

It was Wednesday when we brunched on crepes
in a restaurant high above the Pacific, and we walked
beside the water, watching blossoms
and blades of grass
blown by the wind,
float and drift to earth again.
We talked of traveling, of Stephanie and Chris,
we were attempting sainthood,
trying to comprehend, accept the pain;
such a strange and difficult time

for your mate and mine.
I was trying to understand
but the complexity was far away,
I was with you, I only wanted
to be with you.

It was Wednesday when you took me to a place
that on every city map is called the Filbert Steps
but in my memory is recorded as an uncharted,
enchanted garden, existing only for us,
unforgettable beauty, bower of spring,
reflection of love. Now, I remember
a Saturday when we lay down together for the first time.
We made love again and again, late into the night
curved together in sleep at dawn, only to awaken
to the miracle of our pleasure in each other.
That was a Sunday. I was already afraid
of losing you.

Now it is Wednesday again. The morning drifts by.
Only three hours ago you were in my bed,
we were bathed in tears. I was holding you
naked
against my nakedness for the last time,
tracing the fine lines of your neck, drowning
for one moment more in the valleys of you,
the softness of your skin. I was desperate,
trying to imprint the memory

of your shoulder
deep
into my being.

It is just past ten thirty,
thirty-one, thirty-two, thirty-three,
and I am beginning to cry again.
I stand valiantly at the typewriter, devoted
to language,
to the insistent demand that the inner report
is more important. Put it on paper get it down
make sentences and phrases out of heartbreak,
shape it, carve out the letters and if
you are going to cry out,
articulate the cry,
spill it in poetry,
let your pain and gladness
have a word.

As I leave you at your door
and begin the slow upward
curve of the highway above the water,
the cobalt blue, shining diamonds water,
I am feeling myself expand,
wanting to be more, to live my life
as if I were this ocean,
to have the strength and breadth
of the Golden Gate, to carry whole nations and races

in my arms, shine magnificently
as the sun, to become...what?
It is a moment of exultation without completion.
I become whatever it is I become
without you, my lover, my dream,
without you.

It is Tuesday evening. I prepare coffee.
I roll two cigarettes. I light three candles.
You begin speaking and I already know we are ending.
I listen without comment.
You read the midnight thoughts
locked until this moment in your journal. You weep as you read.
I listen without speaking. I listen without protest.
You are true, your thoughts are true, your writing is true.
You say, "We let our secrets, like birds, out of cages."
Your love your sorrow your understanding
are all finely etched in the black ink
of your handwriting. I listen without speaking.

On my table in the porcelain vase is a bouquet of red roses.
The shadow of the roses on my ceiling forms a canopy over you.
The shadow of the roses listens without speaking.

There are three candles. You are crying. You speak of your pain.
As you say, "I realize now, it is a dynasty of pain,"
one candle goes out.
In the two candles still burning,

I recognize the inevitable:
we must both go back to ourselves,
we divide into two. The triangle is
inevitable, and inevitably it has to die. Somehow I know
if I contemplate the geometric figure of the triangle,
I will understand everything, the theme beneath the love song
the human race sings
will become clear to me in the triangle.
I do not contemplate this.
I am only
listening. Two candles burning.
The shadow of the roses on my ceiling.

Earlier this evening, I understood:
I must let you go, bear the pain,
before your pain erases even the memory
of our love.
You are crying, you are telling me
you must choose yourself now
or be lost.
The shadow of the roses on the ceiling knows.
(The silence of the candlelight, the silence of the shadow.)
The first words I speak
are from a song I heard a long time ago:
"Loving is letting go, a wish to let another grow."

It is Wednesday. We break the bond
of pleasure and pain, we let go.

I am trying
to let go. I know I have been released
from a passion that has gripped me
in its beautiful talons
since early winter, a winter
that was almost spring,
when the fragrant air beckoned me
into your arms. We have been released
from the fire that was consuming us,
burning in ecstasy, drowning in pain.
Our souls and our selves
have had to break from the nuptial center
of our perfect loving, our imperfect
union.

I want to find words to describe
the exact green of this empty bottle of wine
standing upright beside the roses on my table.
The rose petals are a deep red,
the blossoms are full.
The roses will die. The shadow of the roses
will never again
form a canopy
over you.

Sonoma

Chapters

I
I wake from a dream, haven of sleep,
curve of rest, a dream where I find
I am loved
by a strong and lovely woman.
I drive to your house in the night
and arrive at your doorway
still mourning
a love lying in ashes. I knock at your door
not knowing what to say, how to touch you, only here
out of instinct,
following the scent of a secret
I may have always known
but did not have the courage to see
until now, in this gentle, fearful hour of our meeting,
until now, this winter evening.

I enter the house that shelters you and your children
without gifts, without the pride
of a history that schooled me in courting, I am here
with only an unspoken question. Are you
the woman in my dream, the woman
who loves me? And I wonder, if I ask,

oh rare, exquisite
beauty,
will you lie with me?

We are moving slowly in a warm bath of water
beneath the starlight, the distance of the years
that trained us to avert our eyes
is still between us.
Our voices drift for hours in the steam while I wait
to pass through the shyness enveloping me and
the first stroke of your hand on my skin
stops my breath, my muscles begin to ache while I wait
to embrace you.

You are naked and soft, lying above me, borne by the water.
I caress your back, your arms, discover
your hands, your face,
and I wait
wait
in the moonlight and shadow
beside a jungle path,
bone of liquid, sinew of desire, vein of fire,
I wait
to devour you.

You are trembling
in a bed of brilliant crimson colors,
I cannot find an end

to the desire you awaken, we turn and turn
in a satin embrace, our mouths, our tongues,
return again and again to the miracle repeated
in our kisses.

Your sighs wash over me, sound and skin mingle,
your voice calling my name
is the music our passion is creating, your voice
is the source, the fullness, my hands and my tongue
are seeking.

I am a lover without language,
you are a woman whose sweetness I cannot measure,
I want to be here forever, I am surrendering
everything
to the insistent warmth
of your touch.

Your hair is a thick black mane I spread
over my belly
while you drink pleasure from my loins
endlessly
I am dying of ecstasy,
I am reborn
in finding you.

II

Now there are no hours, nor seconds,
only moments, the infinity
between breaths, only moments
I remember now as invisible doorways
I pass through like a ghost,
without body, without protest, I move like water
through these passageways made of
the space between midnight and morning,
doorways lit by dawn light
and the radiance
of your face.

Your face, where a child sleeps, where
a woman is beckoning,
your eyes of Ireland mist and northern blue
skies, obsidian lashes
(the Spaniard in your blood, your lineage remembers
a Mediterranean night.)

I am lost
in looking at you, lost
in the silence and wonder
of lying in your arms, in rest you

reveal your soul of fire and light,
beneath the skin, sagittarian universe
where I am falling, I am following,
without body, without protest,
like a ghost, like water, as the moon descends
and surrenders to sunrise
I descend and surrender,
desire becomes
devotion.

III

Whatever is holy in being human,
in loving, in love, dimension of immortality, flight
to a sacred island,
beyond caution, beyond fear,
almost beyond beauty, this landscape of love
I see in your face
mirrors my content,
an eternity of fulfillment.

Now there are no hours,
nor minutes, nor seconds
only this moment when
we are silent
while our hearts speak

(a seed takes root in our blood,
her tendrils entwine us,
a nightingale in another land
announces the spring
again).

Remembering

Stephanie

I dreamt about you last night.
We talked about music
and I made you a cup of tea.

We went for a walk and you
told me it had been twenty-eight years
since you beat the death sentence
the doctors laid on you.

Twenty-eight years!
How about that?

I put my arm around your waist
and thought how good it was
to feel your body there,
how I used to imagine
I could still embrace my mother
after she was gone.

Then I woke up and remembered,
your body is only real
in my dreams.

That Time We Argued

I was happy, drunk,
when I told the story
of that time we argued.

It was so intense
and you were
furious.
Finally, you ended it by
flinging your fur coat
over one shoulder
and storming out of the house.

You swept by me
with all the majesty and disdain
of a queen,
and I forgot completely
what we had been arguing about.

All I could feel
was the thrill
of being your lover,
all I could think was

oh
my
God
you're beautiful.

Amen

Whenever I hear the opening chords
of Stevie Wonder singing
You are the sunshine of my life...
I think of you, and remember
your wild spirit,
divine madness,
the battle and beauty
of loving you.

Prayer and pain, an ocean of love,
sweet rivers we swam
together.

Dancing in the moonlight, sunlight,
all and everything for God,
all this I remember,
amen.

Fated

I loved you once, so in love with you
I ached for you
even when I was with you.

Our love was lyric, lovely, wild.
You were champagne and cognac,
heady, intoxicating,
becoming an amber warmth
that burned down to my core,
down to a liquid surrender.

It could not last. We were fated to end
even at our beginning.

After Midnight

Those poems I wrote so long ago,
I read again tonight. There it was,
my long lament
that sunlit morning
when we said our final farewell.
I left you and drove along the water's edge,
my heart high because I had loved you,
broken, because I had lost you.

I set the poems aside, and drank hot tea,
dark, fragrant, meant to lull me to sleep.
Instead, it stirred a memory
and remembering,
I felt a need
to find you.

So I looked for you, as any modern woman might,
on the computer. No need for a question, only
your name typed into a narrow frame
of the cyber-universe. And there you were,
older, yes, but with that certain lilt
and lift about you, your dry humor charming an audience

I could not see. They laughed with you
as you read your poems, and told them of turning
your loneliness into absurdity, a country western song
about heartache. We've all been there.
At least, I have.

I felt glad, glad to know you're alive,
and though you are, at times, bereft,
you are able still to be amused by it all;
through all these years, writing,
you have transformed
your griefs and joys into poetry,
giving us
an eloquent, stinging, language of the heart.

I found you, after midnight, and discovered
you are only ninety miles away.
Thank God I no longer love you,
no longer ache for you,
or I would tumble down the road
to lie at your doorway
and weep.

Los Angeles
San Francisco
Corvallis

The Mighty Pen

I believe it is true that the pen
is mightier than the sword.
The sword pierces, slices, brutalizes
and ends life.
The pen records, embraces, immortalizes
our lives and loves,
grief and loss.

These poems about the women I have loved
will outlive me, will still speak
when my lovers and I are silent.
They will last as long as language lasts,
our passion and heartache
will fall from a dusty shelf
in some other era, or filter across a screen
to be read by a forlorn writer
alone at midnight,
stumbling through someone else's memories.

I know about the power of the pen
because I won my beloved
with a poem. Yes, it's true.

I had been courting her for months,
to no avail. We were friends, nothing more.
We spent the evening together,
saw the film Autumn Sonata, then to a café
called the Bicycle Shop.
We sat at a circular table in a crowded room,
and for me, there was no one else there,
only her, no one else. No one.
We drank café royale, an elegant warmth
of brandy in dark, bitter coffee.
Brandy and coffee, smoke and talk,
and finally, I drove her home.
In the driveway, saying good-night,
I told her I had written a poem for her.
She wanted to hear it.
I agreed to read it to her in exchange for a kiss.
That was our bargain.

We went upstairs, and settled in her living room
with one last nightcap. I read the poem to her.
She liked it. I got my kiss. She liked that too.
One kiss led to another, and that was the beginning
of a love story we are still living.

Coda

Final Farewell

Wherever you are,
I hope you are well, and happy.
It was a joy to know you,
laugh with you, love you.

If ever I hurt you,
I ask that you forgive me.
You broke my heart
and I forgive you.

www.ingramcontent.com/pod-product-compliance
Lightning Source LLC
Chambersburg PA
CBHW030458010526
44118CB00011B/1001